5 SECONDS OF SUMMER

BOOK OF STUFF

CON

HELLO AND WELCOME

Hello and welcome to the first ever official 5SOS annual! It's piled high with interviews, quizzes, and a whole load of random facts.

The last year has been an incredible one for the band. They released their debut album, set off on their first ever worldwide tour, played two nights at LA's world-renowned Forum, and have won a whole bunch of awards along the way. The boys even started their own record label and signed a band!

5SOS have got some big plans for the future. So read on and be prepared to be very surprised …

AROUND THE WORLD
WITH 5SOS

The guys share their favorite
memories of world domination …

THE US

ASHTON

I recently went into the desert to the Joshua Tree National Park, which is about two and a half hours' drive from LA. I put The Eagles on the car stereo. We were in a Mustang and the top was down, and driving around in it with the music blaring felt like the coolest thing I'd ever done in my life.

CALUM

Just being on the bus with the crew and going around to different venues on the last tour we did was so cool because you're discovering new places. You can never get bored when you're doing that.

LUKE

The first time we went to the States we went to Miami. We arrived at the airport and didn't really know if we had any fans there. We spotted one girl waiting in the terminal and thought that was it, but as we walked down the escalator there were 300 fans waiting, so we had to hop on one of those airport minicars to get out. It was sad because we didn't meet our fans, but it was still a great experience for our first visit.

MICHAEL

Playing our gig at the LA Forum. I think that's the best one we've ever done. The younger Choice Awards were also cool because we played a pretty heavy song – that was our way of playing a younger show but also being ourselves.

THE UK

ASHTON

The UK's where our band really kicked off and it's like our second home. It was the first place we were signed, and we played all our first real gigs there. We lived in a little house in Ealing in London for nearly a year and that's where we wrote most of our first album. It was also the first place we'd ever seen snow, so I'll never forget that!

CALUM

There was this really funny moment when we were driving in a van on our first trip to London. We all suddenly got out and started messing around with these cones for some reason. It was random, but at the time it was really funny.

LUKE

I think going to Radio 1 and finding out we were number one in the UK with our first single will always stay with me. That was cool. We had a band hug.

MICHAEL

Nando's. Every time I go it's better than the last time. The Nando's we had when I landed a few days ago was the best I've ever had in my life because I hadn't had it in a year.

11

ITALY

LEANING TOWER OF PIZZA

ASHTON

I went to my first rave in Turin and that was insane. It was awesome. I want to go to another one now.

CALUM

We had a signing in the middle of this square that had an incredible cathedral and other amazing buildings. We walked out on the balcony and there was a sea of people there to see us. That blew me away.

LUKE

Obviously the spaghetti and mozzarella are great! We did a signing and there were stacks of kids everywhere. It was in a famous square in Italy and we walked out onto a balcony and all you could see were the fans down below, like three or four thousand of them. I'd never seen so many fans in one place like that before.

MICHAEL

The food – because it's amazing. It's the best food in the world, I think. I love Italian food.

JAPAN

ASHTON

I really love the fashion there because they have a really cool rock style. They also massively love music and still buy it in physical form, because they love the passion that surrounds the artwork. If you haven't done a good job on the artwork, they won't buy it, and I think that's so cool.

CALUM

We went to this robot show and it was the weirdest but most fascinating thing I'd ever seen in my life. Japan's like a different world. The technology over there is awesome.

LUKE

We went to the robot restaurant in Japan and that was amazing. Japan is very loud and really buzzy everywhere.

MICHAEL

Going to the arcades. I probably stayed in those arcades for three days straight.

AUSTRALIA

ASHTON

Playing in Australia feels really different to anywhere else in the world, because it's our home. There's a sense of ownership over our band there and it feels really nice to play shows for them. We can also make a lot more Australian jokes, because they get it more than anywhere else in the world!

CALUM

The first time we went into a studio with the band was awesome – we were so naïve but we all had a great time. I'll always remember that.

LUKE

I always think back to the start of the band. We didn't have a clue what we were doing and we were so naïve and just having a really good time. We had no idea it was all about to kick off.

MICHAEL

My favorite memory is probably our first show. It was the first time we'd played a gig as a band and it was weird, because we thought there were going to be loads of people coming along . . . but only twelve people turned up. It was still awesome because we played on a stage and we loved it.

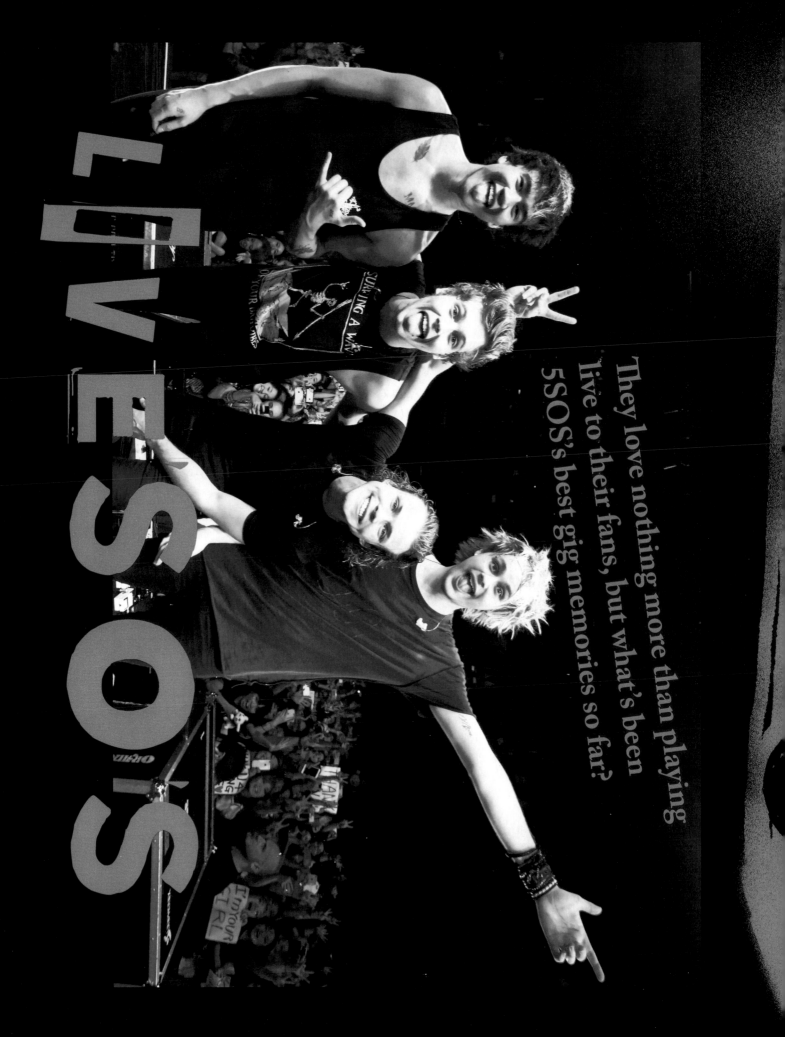

LIVE 5SOS

They love nothing more than playing live to their fans, but what's been 5SOS's best gig memories so far?

What have been 5SOS's best gig memories so far?

ASHTON

I probably have a different answer every day. There was one we did at the Stade de France that was awesome. I love Coldplay and their live album was recorded there, so it was a really great thing to play there too. The other one that was amazing was the one we did at the Roxy LA, which was a brilliant gig for me and the boys. It was a time when we were happy with how we sounded as a band – the fans really started to understand us and who we are and what we want to do with our music. That felt like a real turning point.

CALUM

The LA Forum was our first headline arena show and all our parents came over to the States and saw it. I guess until that moment our parents were only 80 percent sure about the band. They weren't really sure if we were doing anything big because we were always away, and they don't hear much from us. But that kind of showed them that we were actually doing something with our lives!

LUKE

Probably the Forum gig we did in LA. It was our first big headline arena show with full production and pyro and everything. That was a big moment for us. To be able to play in front of that many people was incredible, and we did two nights there.

MICHAEL

The Forum in LA. It was our first arena show and the biggest show we'd played to date. It kind of felt like everything we'd done had built up to that massive show with the pyro and our families there and everything. That was really special. I wish we'd filmed it.

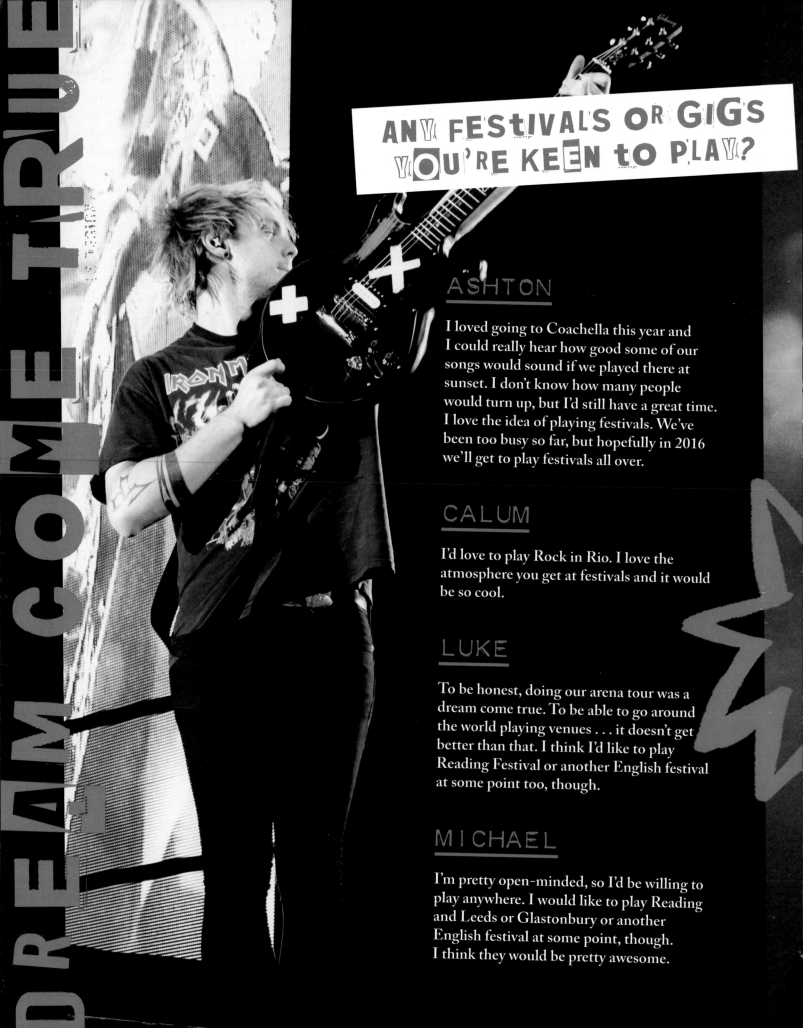

DREAM COME TRUE

ANY FESTIVALS OR GIGS YOU'RE KEEN TO PLAY?

ASHTON

I loved going to Coachella this year and I could really hear how good some of our songs would sound if we played there at sunset. I don't know how many people would turn up, but I'd still have a great time. I love the idea of playing festivals. We've been too busy so far, but hopefully in 2016 we'll get to play festivals all over.

CALUM

I'd love to play Rock in Rio. I love the atmosphere you get at festivals and it would be so cool.

LUKE

To be honest, doing our arena tour was a dream come true. To be able to go around the world playing venues . . . it doesn't get better than that. I think I'd like to play Reading Festival or another English festival at some point too, though.

MICHAEL

I'm pretty open-minded, so I'd be willing to play anywhere. I would like to play Reading and Leeds or Glastonbury or another English festival at some point, though. I think they would be pretty awesome.

IS BIGGER BETTER?

CALUM

The smaller gigs are definitely more intimate. The crowd sees everything you do, whereas in arenas you can't really see everything, so actions and your personality have to be a lot bigger on stage. But I really enjoy both, to be fair.

LUKE

Obviously I like playing arenas, but I'd like to keep playing small club gigs too so we don't lose that side of who we are. We're here because of those small, sweaty club gigs, so I'd like to keep doing them no matter how big we get.

ASHTON

As a musician it's a massive learning curve going from smaller venues to arenas, just because whatever you thought you knew about playing your instrument totally changes. It's completely different from playing theaters and clubs, and that's a great thing to learn at such a young age. Once you're playing at arena standard your recordings improve so much, and that's such a blessing. We get to make better music just from having the experience of playing bigger places. Also, learning how to perform and entertain 20,000 people is a really cool thing to do when it's something you dream about as a kid.

MICHAEL

I think I'd be stupid to say I don't miss playing smaller venues. Big venues are amazing because we can play to more of our fans and it shows that our fan base has grown. But there is a sort of energy that's missing in bigger venues that you can only get by doing those small, sweaty places. I don't think we're ever going to stop doing those small shows. We could be playing somewhere massive one day, but the night before we might perform for 300 people. We'll always want to keep that closeness.

We asked Ashton some questions. He very kindly answered them.

ALIENS ARRIVE ON EARTH WHO'VE NEVER HEARD OF YOU. HOW WOULD YOU DESCRIBE THE BAND TO THEM?

I would describe us as four individuals in a type of group that makes music together, which is a band. And then I would tell them that I'm the drummer, and there's a guitarist and another guitarist and a bass guitarist, and we attempt to make people happy with music.

DO YOU HAVE ANY NICKNAMES FOR EACH OTHER?

Not really, we just stick to Cal, Mike, Luke, and Ash. We keep it pretty simple. I don't think Michael even likes to be called Mike, but he got over that a few years ago.

WHAT'S THE LAST THING YOU DO BEFORE YOU GO ON STAGE?

I brush my teeth. We all brush our teeth together. It's really weird, but it means that we're minty fresh for the stage.

WHICH OF THE AWARDS YOU'VE WON ARE YOU MOST PROUD OF?

We won an Australian award called an APRA songwriting award, which meant a lot to us. For people in the industry to recognize that we put a lot of effort into our songwriting was amazing. I think a lot of people get sidetracked because we're young and they might not think we write a lot of our stuff, but we write every single word and every piece of music. So it was really cool to receive an award for songwriting, especially from our home country. Every single award that we've won so far is basically for the fans. They make everything happen and they make us look good.

IS THERE AN AWARD YOU'D LIKE TO WIN?

I've no idea – I haven't thought about awards too much. It's definitely not my mind-set. It's a cool thing that happens and I appreciate it, but it's not my focus. I look forward to meeting other bands at award shows and I think they're really fun, but winning is just a cool thing that comes with it.

DO YOU EVER GET NERVOUS ABOUT PERFORMING, AND IF SO, HOW DO YOU DEAL WITH IT?

I don't get nervous at all, really. I think at some point when you're a performer nerves just turn into excitement. I kind of chill out. I am what I am and I do what I do on stage, and getting nervous isn't going to change anything. Although, having said that, sometimes during the first show on tour I get a little nervous because if you mess up when you're the drummer it's very noticeable, and I want to put on the best show possible.

WHAT ADVICE WOULD YOU GIVE TO FANS WHO WANT TO START THEIR OWN BAND?

No matter how many people you start a band with, you have to pay attention to each other's strengths and individual characteristics.

WHAT DO YOU GUYS FALL OUT ABOUT?

We're surprisingly really close and we never fight or anything like that. We have a strange way of communicating that I don't think other people understand. We're definitely best friends, and even if I go away somewhere without them, when I come back it's like I never left.

19

WHAT'S THE MOST ROCK 'N' ROLL THING YOU'VE EVER DONE?

I've trashed a few drum kits, but I don't know if that's rock 'n' roll. I mean, there's always the occasional bit of blood on the drum kit from my hands after I've been playing, but I've never thrown any TVs out of windows or anything. Mainly because TVs are heavy and expensive.

WHAT'S YOUR FAVORITE 5SOS LYRIC?

It's probably in "Beside You": "When we both fall asleep beneath the same sky / To the beat of our heart at the same time." That's a cool lyric about missing someone.

WHAT'S YOUR GO-TO COMFORT FOOD?

I love fish and chips. I've also discovered a newfound love for waffles, having been in the States so much. Waffles are so good. Denny's Diner rules. That's the best place in the world for any comfort food, ever.

WHO DO YOU CALL WHEN YOU'RE BORED?

I always text my mum. She always listens to whatever I have to say and she doesn't judge me. I've really developed a cool friendship with my mum since growing a little older. I didn't really understand her when I was younger, but we get on really well now. Or I'll text my uncle. He's a really cool dude. He's a heart surgeon and always doing exciting things that take my mind off wherever we're at for a moment.

WHAT'S NEXT FOR THE BAND?

Our next album is coming out and we'll be touring endlessly and going everywhere we can. We'll hopefully get to do a lot of the artwork and things on the album too. It would be great for people to see and understand who we are individually a little more. We've grown since the last album and the new songs are going to sound brilliant live, so I hope people will want to come and see us perform them!

HOW DO YOU DEAL WITH JET LAG?

I never look at what time it is where I've come from and I just get on with my day. I also never nap and I make sure I don't go to sleep before 10pm wherever I've gone so I can get back into a routine.

WHAT DID YOU DO LAST NIGHT?

I went and spoke about the new album with all our London mates and just hung out with the band.

ARE THERE ANY OTHER INSTRUMENTS YOU'D LIKE TO LEARN?

I'd like to learn every instrument – I love them all. They're like different languages and I could never know enough of them.

CAN YOU SPEAK ANY OTHER LANGUAGE?

I can't, sadly. Learning Italian or French would be cool. I tried some Japanese when we went to Japan but my mouth doesn't seem to work that way, so I don't think I'd be great.

I'VE TRASHED
A FEW DRUM KITS

THE ULTIMATE 5SOS
PLAYLIST

Elevate – **St. Lucia**

Warning – **Green Day**

Road Trippin' – **Red Hot Chili Peppers**

You're Not Alone – **Saosin**

Empty Apartment – **Yellowcard**

Asthenia – **Blink 182**

To Live and Let Go – **All Time Low**

If These Sheets Were States – **All Time Low**

Everything's Magic – **Angels and Airwaves**

A Sky Full of Stars – **Coldplay**

In Too Deep – **Sum 41**

23

WHAT I LIKE ABOUT YOU

Here are some of the reasons why 5SOS are fans of their fans

ASHTON

A fan bought us a star once. A legitimate star. I think we owned it for about a month, and it had the coordinates on it and everything. It was registered as the 5SOS star, so that was pretty cool. I just hope it wasn't too expensive!

CALUM

A fan wanted to give me a bass, but I was leaving to go to the airport and couldn't really take it with me because I felt like it would break. What an amazing present, though.

LUKE

Once when a fan gave us some art we turned it into merch, and that was really cool. We get given some really amazing fan art that must have taken ages to do.

MICHAEL

Someone bought me an old-school Game Boy once. I'd lost mine and then she gave me a new one, which was crazy.

25

Fancy answering some questions, Calum? You do? Much appreciated.

ALIENS ARRIVE ON EARTH WHO'VE NEVER HEARD OF YOU. HOW WOULD YOU DESCRIBE THE BAND TO THEM?

A classical quartet with rock upbringings. I'd keep it pretty simple.

DO YOU HAVE ANY NICKNAMES FOR EACH OTHER?

Not really, I just shorten the names. So Ashton is Ash and Michael is Mike and Luke is . . . Luke! I guess I'm Cal, but we haven't thought about it too much. We haven't created anything new.

WHAT'S THE LAST THING YOU DO BEFORE YOU GO ON STAGE?

We fist-bump our whole crew.

WHICH OF THE AWARDS YOU'VE WON ARE YOU MOST PROUD OF?

We got an award for Breakthrough Songwriter of the Year from APRA in Australia, and that hit me hard because I remember writing these really bad songs in my room when I was fifteen. To be able to have that award shows a lot of progression, so it's really close to my heart.

IS THERE AN AWARD YOU'D LIKE TO WIN?

Not really. I feel like awards are just the perks of being in a band if you're good enough, so I don't aim to win them as such.

DO YOU EVER GET NERVOUS ABOUT PERFORMING, AND IF SO, HOW DO YOU DEAL WITH IT?

I don't get nervous anymore. I was nervous during our Forum show in LA, so it's really just the big ones I worry about. But you kind of get used to the nerves and it becomes more like excitement. It's a very relaxed atmosphere backstage, so that's good for the nerves.

WHAT ADVICE WOULD YOU GIVE TO FANS WHO WANT TO START THEIR OWN BAND?

Find a group of friends you really enjoy playing music with and don't listen to anyone who's negative towards you. Songwrite heaps and practice heaps and work hard. A lot of people alienated us at school because we were doing these really small tours and they didn't believe in us, but we kept at it. We didn't let anything put us off.

WHAT DO YOU GUYS FALL OUT ABOUT?

We very rarely fall out. It's a very open band and if we have something to say then we say it. We don't want to become a band where we have all these grudges in twenty years' time. I feel like everyone is very understanding and nobody has a big ego or anything, which is good.

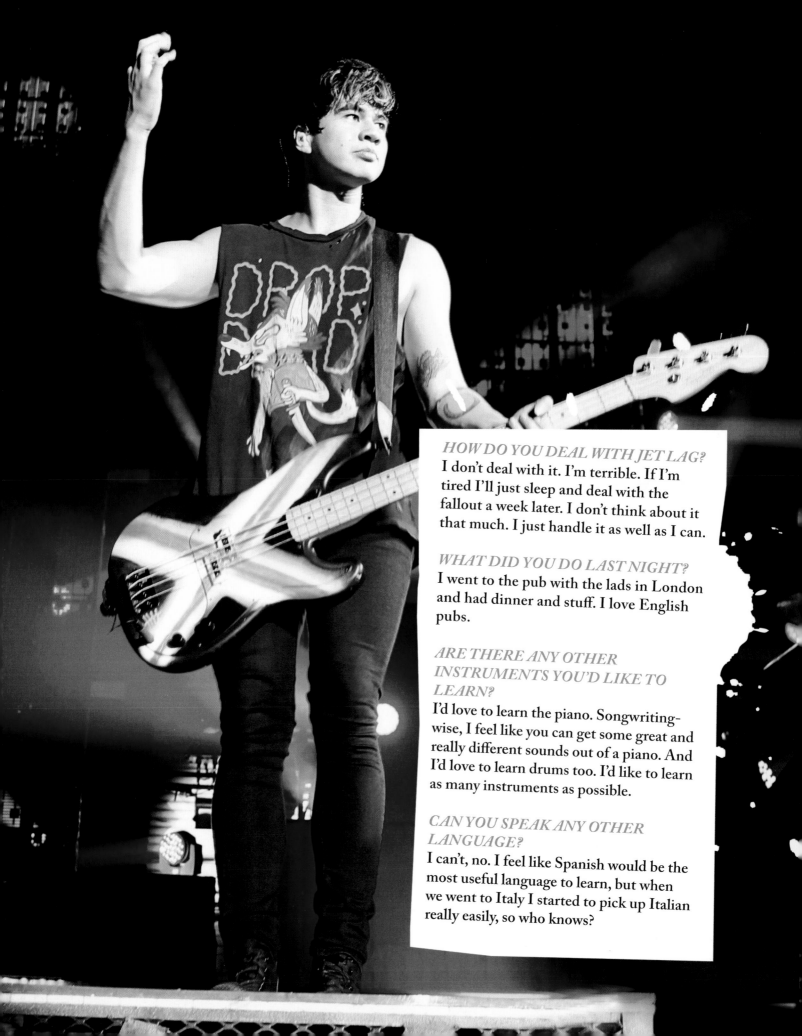

HOW DO YOU DEAL WITH JET LAG?

I don't deal with it. I'm terrible. If I'm tired I'll just sleep and deal with the fallout a week later. I don't think about it that much. I just handle it as well as I can.

WHAT DID YOU DO LAST NIGHT?

I went to the pub with the lads in London and had dinner and stuff. I love English pubs.

ARE THERE ANY OTHER INSTRUMENTS YOU'D LIKE TO LEARN?

I'd love to learn the piano. Songwriting-wise, I feel like you can get some great and really different sounds out of a piano. And I'd love to learn drums too. I'd like to learn as many instruments as possible.

CAN YOU SPEAK ANY OTHER LANGUAGE?

I can't, no. I feel like Spanish would be the most useful language to learn, but when we went to Italy I started to pick up Italian really easily, so who knows?

WHAT'S THE MOST ROCK 'N' ROLL THING YOU'VE EVER DONE?
I am the least rock 'n' roll person *ever*.

WHAT'S YOUR FAVORITE 5SOS LYRIC?
Probably something in "Disconnected": "Tune out the static sound of the city that never sleeps / Here in the moment on the dark side of the screen."

WHAT'S YOUR GO-TO COMFORT FOOD?
I like pasta. Specifically, my mum's pasta.

WHO DO YOU CALL WHEN YOU'RE BORED?
I don't really call many people. I'm not a caller. I'm from the generation where it's all about texting. But when I'm back home I usually call one of the band.

WHAT'S NEXT FOR THE BAND?
I'm not sure. I hope we're going to be touring and writing *a lot*. I'm so excited about the next album; it's going to be great. We weren't sure if we were going to beat the first album, but I think we have.

DERP CON

The first ever 5SOS conference brought together giant animals, Pokémon, and, above all, music lovers from around the world.

Fans from across the globe got the opportunity to enter a competition to win the ultimate prize. Not only did they win flights to LA along with a friend, they were also put up in a plush hotel and got to swing by to watch 5SOS perform at LA's world-renowned Forum. And it went off . . .

Derp Con was totally incredible. What's your best memory from it?..

LUKE

I remember looking into the crowd at one point and seeing all these ridiculous animals. There was, like, a lobster or something. These life-sized animals and cartoon characters were scattered through the crowds watching us play. That image in my head is pretty funny. There were people from countries around the world, including places we'd never been to, and our parents were there too, which was really nice.

MICHAEL

I've got a lot of weird memories. There was a huge 8-foot-tall turkey and Raphael from Teenage Mutant Ninja Turtles walking around. Fans from all over the world had come to hang out. I vividly remember those girls dressed like Ash and Pikachu from Pokémon who did the play. It was awesome that they'd spent so long thinking about it and planning it.

ASHTON

I've got so many. There were two fans who came dressed as Pokémon characters. They played out a scene as their characters for at least ten minutes, and it was weird but cool. The whole thing was surreal but amazing. We got to hang out with so many of our fans.

CALUM

I just loved meeting everyone. We met some really cool fans from India – I'd no idea people over there were into our music. Meeting so many fans from different countries was pretty overwhelming. I'd love to go back and do it all again.

31

WHO'S SAID WHAT?

CAN YOU TELL WHICH OF THE GUYS POSTED THESE TWEETS?

1 I simply came here to party.
16 APR 2015; 12: 11

2 I love music, it has a voice for every walk of life, every emotion, every bit of love & heartache, every adventure, it speaks like nothing else.
17 APR 2015; 06: 05

3 Has anyone seen a blue whale? Pls tell me what it was like.
9 APR 2015; 21: 59

4 Having a conversation about what brand of tea I like. 27 MAR 2015; 01: 39

5 No matter how nasty people are in life ... Show kindness, smile through it and love, laugh, be good people, just cause you can ... 25 FEB 2015; 12: 28

6 Someone just said I have a big head, literally
26 APR 2015; 20: 45

7 If there's one thing I lose sleep on its why I can never beat Luke at ping pong 19 FEB 2015; 04: 06

8 In need of a burrito 18 MAR 2015; 02: 48

9 I wanna little bit of California, with a little bit of London sky 10 MAR 2015; 08: 47

10 I love animals, they are the most beautiful peaceful things in the world
27 MAR 2015; 19: 05

11 Yiiiiiiiieeeeeeeeeew 16 APR 2015; 12: 15

12 Eating mcdonalds watching Netflix on valentines day. what's happened to me
14 FEB 2015; 01: 23

13 We're 4 of the luckiest kids in the world and its thanks to all of our amazing supporters
16 NOV 2014; 09: 09

14 A bee landed on my face and then flew off, my life flashed before my eyes
21 JAN 2015; 04: 47

Luke was kind enough to answer some questions for us. He's good like that.

ALIENS ARRIVE ON EARTH WHO'VE NEVER HEARD OF YOU. HOW WOULD YOU DESCRIBE THE BAND TO THEM?

I'd describe us as four dudes who grew up in not the best area of Sydney and started jamming together for fun. We're a pop-rock band. We all sing, there are two guitars, a bass, and drums. I'd probably mention our favorite bands like Green Day and Blink 182 and say we're a bit like them, but a newer version.

DO YOU HAVE ANY NICKNAMES FOR EACH OTHER?

I sometimes call Ashton "Irwin" because, er, that's his last name. Then it's Mikey for Michael and Cal for Calum.

WHAT'S THE LAST THING YOU DO BEFORE YOU GO ON STAGE?

I usually fist-bump the band or maybe yell something and make a loud noise.

WHICH OF THE AWARDS YOU'VE WON ARE YOU MOST PROUD OF?

Winning New Artist of the Year at the American Music Awards was pretty cool. We've also won an APRA for Breakthrough Songwriter of the Year in Australia and that was cool.

IS THERE AN AWARD YOU'D LIKE TO WIN?

I'd like to win something to do with live performance, because we pride ourselves on that so much. We've always wanted to be recognized as a great live band.

DO YOU EVER GET NERVOUS ABOUT PERFORMING, AND IF SO, HOW DO YOU DEAL WITH IT?

I probably get nervous at the first or second show of a tour, but not really after that. I may get nervous at a TV show, especially if it's live and not a natural gig environment. I think being in a band kind of helps in that you're not by yourself. I think I would struggle to carry the stage on my own if I was very nervous, but in 5SOS I've got three other dudes to rely on, so that pressure is split.

WHAT ADVICE WOULD YOU GIVE TO FANS WHO WANT TO START THEIR OWN BAND?

Play a lot of live gigs before you've even released any songs. Playing live is what we did *a lot* of in the early days. And just getting along with your band all the time is so important. The tighter you are, the better you are.

WHAT DO YOU GUYS FALL OUT ABOUT?

It's usually only about music and rehearsals. You kind of have to learn to live with these other three people and it'd be terrible if you didn't get on. You kind of know what each other likes and doesn't like at this point, so that makes it a lot easier.

HOW DO YOU DEAL WITH JET LAG?

Eating *a lot.*

WHAT DID YOU DO LAST NIGHT?

We had dinner with some of our managers and then got some sleep.

ARE THERE ANY OTHER INSTRUMENTS YOU'D LIKE TO LEARN?

I can play piano a bit, but I want to get better at it. There are a lot more songs I'd like to learn.

WHAT'S THE MOST ROCK 'N' ROLL THING YOU'VE EVER DONE?

Stayed up past my bedtime!

CAN YOU SPEAK ANY LANGUAGES?

I can speak a sentence in Spanish and a few words in French, but that's about it. Oh, and I speak Australian too.

WHAT'S YOUR FAVORITE 5SOS LYRIC?

Maybe "Take me back to the middle of nowhere," which is from a song called "Long Way from Home."

WHAT'S YOUR GO-TO COMFORT FOOD?

Nachos. Always.

WHO DO YOU CALL WHEN YOU'RE BORED?

I usually FaceTime one of the other boys.

WHAT'S NEXT FOR THE BAND?

We've just finished recording and writing the second album, which is incredible. I can't believe that's actually happened. We'll do our big arena tour, and then we'll tour again! I don't know where that'll be or if it'll be in small clubs or bigger venues after the second album. We'll just keep doing what we're doing.

SCREEN STARS

HOW IMPORTANT ARE THE VIDEOS TO YOU?

MICHAEL: Videos have been a massive thing for us so far. Back in the day people used to put lots of time and effort into theirs and everyone got really excited about them. We're trying to bring that back by always doing something different.

CALUM: We're trying to revive the excitement around them generally. We really love being heavily involved in the whole process, directing them and then seeing what we've created.

ASHTON: Videos are so crucial. They set the whole tone and trend for what you're doing at the time.

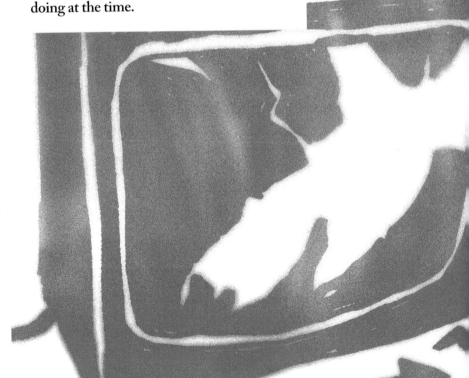

WHAT'S THE PROCESS LIKE WHEN YOU'RE COMING UP WITH IDEAS?

MICHAEL: We usually pitch our ideas to directors and they come back with all of their ideas and we vibe off that. We say what we think would be cool and how we can make it better. It's a kind of back-and-forth process between us and the director.

LUKE: After we've written the song we always spend a lot of time trying to get the concept of the video right before we go on and do it. We'll always have a creative role in everything – especially Ashton, because he loves that side of things. We'll talk with the director and share our ideas.

SO YOU ALWAYS WANT TO MAKE YOUR VIDEOS AN EVENT, BASICALLY?

ASHTON: Totally. I remember getting so excited about other bands' videos coming out, like, ten years ago. I still remember my favorite videos of my favorite bands, and we want people to feel the same about ours. It's been cool to develop ideas and collaborate with brilliant people. I'm really proud of what we've done.

IS THERE ANYTHING YOU HAVEN'T DONE YET THAT YOU'D LIKE TO DO, VIDEO-WISE?

ASHTON: There's always something. My mind's constantly ticking over with ideas. We've got some cool ones coming up for the next album. We've already started talking about them and it's going to be so good.
CALUM: Like Ashton says, we already have a few ideas for the next album that are really exciting.
MICHAEL: Watch this space.

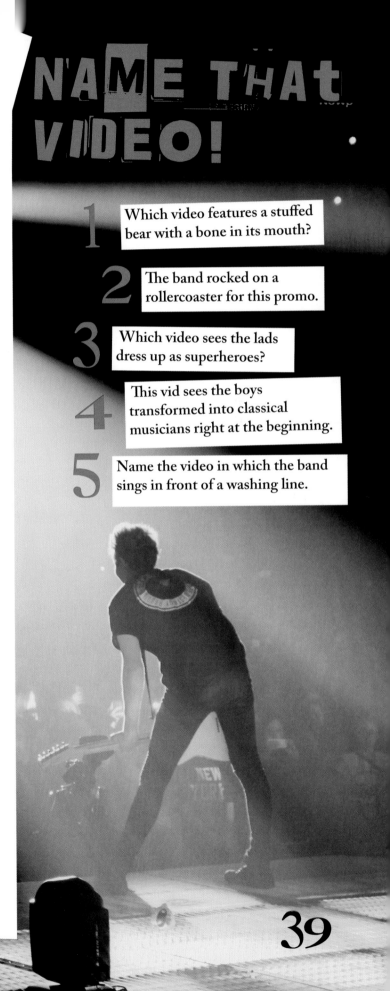

NAME THAT VIDEO!

1 Which video features a stuffed bear with a bone in its mouth?

2 The band rocked on a rollercoaster for this promo.

3 Which video sees the lads dress up as superheroes?

4 This vid sees the boys transformed into classical musicians right at the beginning.

5 Name the video in which the band sings in front of a washing line.

SETLIST, BABY!

rOCK OUT with YOur SOCKS Out

END UP HERE
OUT OF MY LIMIT
HEARTBREAK GIRL
VOODOO DOLL
PERMANENT VACATION
DON'T STOP
DISCONNECTED
LONG WAY HOME
REJECTS
HEARTACHE ON THE BIG SCREEN
WRAPPED AROUND YOUR FINGER
AMNESIA
BESIDE YOU
EVERYTHING I DIDN'T SAY
AMERICAN IDIOT
KISS ME KISS ME
SHE LOOKS SO PERFECT
GOOD GIRLS
WHAT I LIKE ABOUT YOU

MICHAEL

Oi, Michael. Answer some questions for us, will you?

ALIENS ARRIVE ON EARTH WHO'VE NEVER HEARD OF YOU. HOW WOULD YOU DESCRIBE THE BAND TO THEM?

Are they scary aliens? If they're scary I'd tell them that we're the saviors of the human race. If they're nice aliens I'd tell them we're nice to hang out with. I'd like to hang out with aliens, because I'm a bit of an alien guy.

DO YOU HAVE ANY NICKNAMES FOR EACH OTHER?

I call Calum C-Dizzle. Ashton once promised that if we ever sell 40 million albums he'll change his name to Ashtonio. That's an actual thing. That's the only reason we want to keep making music!

WHAT'S THE LAST THING YOU DO BEFORE YOU GO ON STAGE?

Bro-fist everyone and brush our teeth.

WHICH OF THE AWARDS YOU'VE WON ARE YOU MOST PROUD OF?

Our AMA, which we got for Best New Artist. We were up against the biggest artists of last year, like Sam Smith and Iggy Azalea. When I was a kid there was no way I'd ever think we'd win something like that. The best award to look at is the Teen Choice Award, because it's a massive surfboard and looks really cool.

IS THERE AN AWARD YOU'D LIKE TO WIN?

Well, everyone wants to win a Grammy. I'd also like to win a BRIT one day. I want to win *everything*. If there's something to win, I want to win it.

DO YOU EVER GET NERVOUS ABOUT PERFORMING, AND IF SO, HOW DO YOU DEAL WITH IT?

I only get nervous when we do TV shows, because it's not always our fans who are in the audience. Someone like Justin Timberlake could be sitting there and there could be loads of people who are there for him. I don't get nervous when we do our live shows, though, because our fans have always been supportive. I just man up and do it.

WHAT ADVICE WOULD YOU GIVE TO FANS WHO WANT TO START THEIR OWN BAND?

Do it. That's my only advice. Just do it. It's fun. Even before we were successful it was still fun.

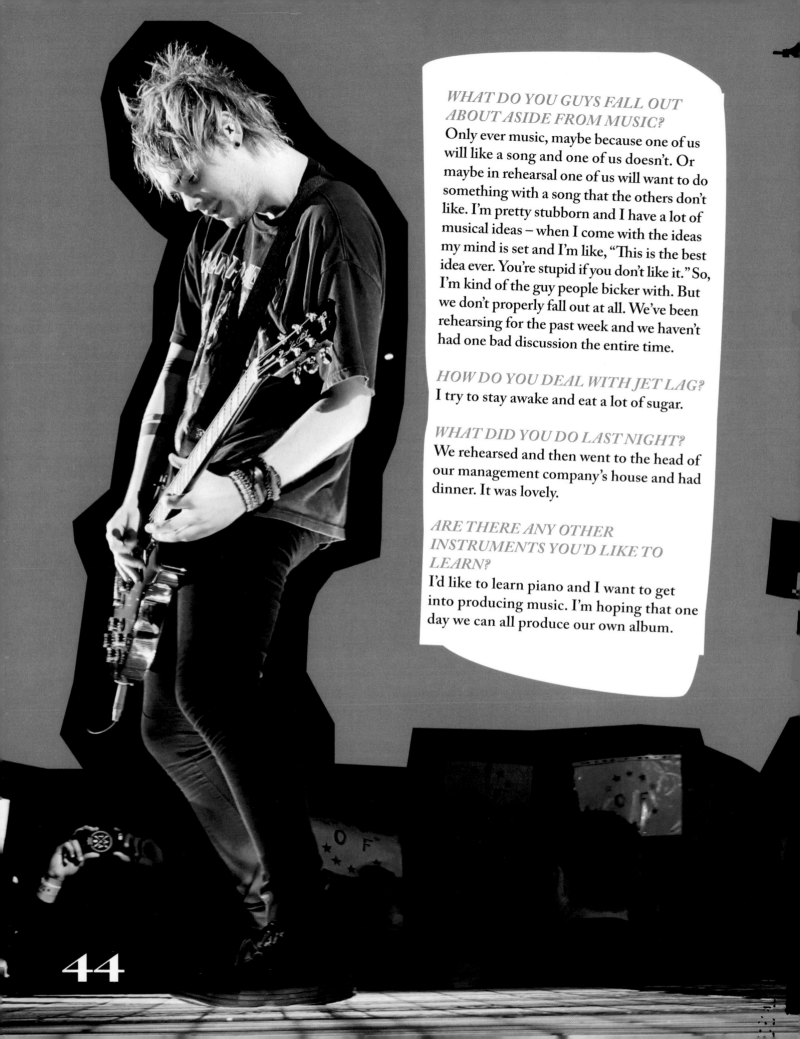

WHAT DO YOU GUYS FALL OUT ABOUT ASIDE FROM MUSIC?

Only ever music, maybe because one of us will like a song and one of us doesn't. Or maybe in rehearsal one of us will want to do something with a song that the others don't like. I'm pretty stubborn and I have a lot of musical ideas – when I come with the ideas my mind is set and I'm like, "This is the best idea ever. You're stupid if you don't like it." So, I'm kind of the guy people bicker with. But we don't properly fall out at all. We've been rehearsing for the past week and we haven't had one bad discussion the entire time.

HOW DO YOU DEAL WITH JET LAG?

I try to stay awake and eat a lot of sugar.

WHAT DID YOU DO LAST NIGHT?

We rehearsed and then went to the head of our management company's house and had dinner. It was lovely.

ARE THERE ANY OTHER INSTRUMENTS YOU'D LIKE TO LEARN?

I'd like to learn piano and I want to get into producing music. I'm hoping that one day we can all produce our own album.

WHAT'S THE MOST ROCK 'N' ROLL THING YOU'VE EVER DONE?

Go to bed at 9:30 pm, which is way past my bedtime. We're so un-rock 'n' roll, we put the Disney Channel to shame. I've always wanted to say I've thrown a TV out of a window, so maybe I should. But I know I'd apologize straight afterwards.

CAN YOU SPEAK ANY OTHER LANGUAGES?

I started to learn Japanese and then I stopped because I realized how hard it is. At first I was like, "Yeah, I can do this!" and then I was like, "This is going to take me a very long time." So no, I can't. But hey, I tried!

WHAT'S YOUR FAVORITE 5SOS LYRIC?

"You were mine for the night / I was out of my mind."

WHAT'S YOUR GO-TO COMFORT FOOD?

I'll go for ice cream. All of the flavors at once.

WHO DO YOU CALL WHEN YOU'RE BORED?

Nobody, really. I'm not really a phone-call kind of guy. I'm more of a go-to-sleep kind of guy. If I was going to call anyone I'd probably call my mum and dad.

WHAT'S NEXT FOR THE BAND?

We're so young and we've still got time to create lots more albums. I think our next album is going to be a real stepping-stone for us, and for our fans as well. We've got lots of new ideas; it's going to be really special. I can't wait for people to hear it. We're more mature as people and as musicians, so lyrically and musically it's more challenging. We're trying to change the game up a little.

BAND MEMBERS

NOT ONLY ARE THEY ONE OF THE WORLD'S BIGGEST BANDS, 5SOS ARE ALSO CHAMPIONING NEW ONES THROUGH THEIR OWN RECORD LABEL, HI OR HEY RECORDS.

BAND MAKER'S

THE LOGO IS VERY COOL

ASHTON: Thanks! I think a good label starts with a type of flag, which was the Hi or Hey Records logo. You kind of see it and go, "Oh, I know what that is." Fans can look at the Hi or Hey stamp on anything and know it comes from us. That really means something to them, which means a lot to us.

TELL US A BIT ABOUT HI OR HEY RECORDS

LUKE: The label is a partnership with Capitol Records. As well as releasing all of our music through it, we wanted it to be a label our fans could be a part of and somewhere we could sign new acts we love. We kind of started it so we could keep close to our fans as the band gets bigger. We want to have the fans as the record-label executives, so to speak.

CALUM: We initially started the label so our fans could feel in control of what we do. A band is more than just music – it's a whole creative cycle.

HAVING YOUR OWN LABEL MUST FEEL INCREDIBLE

CALUM: It does. When we first joined the band we were opened up to so many opportunities, but we didn't know how many of them would be realistic, like starting our own label. Now we have and it feels like it still hasn't sunk in yet.

47

AND THE LABEL ISN'T JUST ABOUT 5SOS ...

MICHAEL: Absolutely not. As soon as we set up the label we figured out what we wanted to do with it, which is sign a band and take them on tour with us. At the beginning of 2015 we signed our first act, the amazing Hey Violet, and the feedback we've had already has been incredible. The band is made up of three girls, Miranda, Nia, and Rena, and one guy, Casey. We love them and we hope all our fans will love them. They're almost a girl band, but then they've got this cool twist of having a guy in there. Sometimes people call them "The girls" and then Casey is like, "Erm, hi!" Their sound is like pop punk and high energy, and they remind us of what we were like when we first started out.

WHAT WAS IT ABOUT HEY VIOLET THAT REALLY STOOD OUT?

ASHTON: We'd always dreamed of finding a band with similar characteristics to us but also really different somehow, and then these punk-rock-type girls with colorful hair came along. We were really looking for a girl band, but we wanted girls who would be role models. I think it's important for girls to have strong people to look up to. I think in this day and age all bands are made up of boys, so we wanted something really new. It's a really cool thing they're doing.

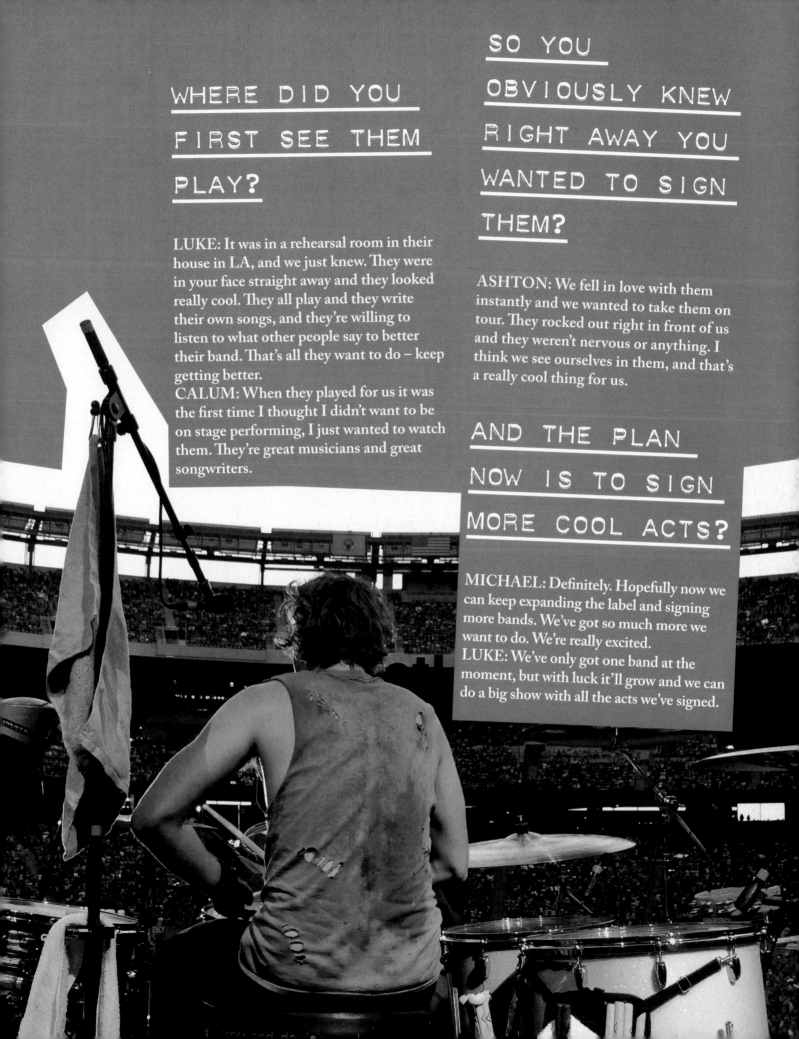

WHERE DID YOU FIRST SEE THEM PLAY?

LUKE: It was in a rehearsal room in their house in LA, and we just knew. They were in your face straight away and they looked really cool. They all play and they write their own songs, and they're willing to listen to what other people say to better their band. That's all they want to do – keep getting better.

CALUM: When they played for us it was the first time I thought I didn't want to be on stage performing, I just wanted to watch them. They're great musicians and great songwriters.

SO YOU OBVIOUSLY KNEW RIGHT AWAY YOU WANTED TO SIGN THEM?

ASHTON: We fell in love with them instantly and we wanted to take them on tour. They rocked out right in front of us and they weren't nervous or anything. I think we see ourselves in them, and that's a really cool thing for us.

AND THE PLAN NOW IS TO SIGN MORE COOL ACTS?

MICHAEL: Definitely. Hopefully now we can keep expanding the label and signing more bands. We've got so much more we want to do. We're really excited.

LUKE: We've only got one band at the moment, but with luck it'll grow and we can do a big show with all the acts we've signed.

QUICKFIRE

The big issues keeping you awake at night

LUKE

CAT OR DOG?
Dog.

BEST PIZZA TOPPING?
Pepperoni.

WHAT COLOR ARE YOUR SOCKS?
Black.

HOW MANY TATTOOS DO YOU HAVE?
I don't have any tattoos. I'd like to but I'm too indecisive.

CAN YOU DRIVE?
I can drive in Australia as of September 2014.

MICHAEL

CAT OR DOG?
Dog.

BEST PIZZA TOPPING?
Pepperoni.

WHAT COLOR ARE YOUR SOCKS?
Black.

HOW MANY TATTOOS DO YOU HAVE?
Seven

CAN YOU DRIVE?
No, but I hope I'll be able to soon.

CALUM

CAT OR DOG?
Dog, every time.

BEST PIZZA TOPPING?
Ham and pineapple.

WHAT COLOR ARE YOUR SOCKS?
Black.

HOW MANY TATTOOS DO YOU HAVE?
I think it's eight now. Is that right?

CAN YOU DRIVE?
No, but I'd like to eventually.

ASHTON

CAT OR DOG?
Dog, for sure.

BEST PIZZA TOPPING?
I love a margarita. I'm a basic dude.

WHAT COLOR ARE YOUR SOCKS?
Today, they're black.

HOW MANY TATTOOS DO YOU HAVE?
nly have one and it's of one of our band's logos.

CAN YOU DRIVE?
an kind of drive. I'm not very good because I
d to leave the country when I was seventeen,
I didn't get my full licence. But I'll get there
one day.

5SOS ON 5SOS

Some very important questions that need answering

WHO WAS THE CUTEST BABY?

ASHTON: Probably Calum. He definitely has the cute-baby genes. His dad's from Scotland and his mum's from New Zealand, and that makes for a cute baby.

LUKE: I'd like to say me, but I've seen Calum as a baby and his cheeks are the cutest cheeks ever.

CALUM: I'd agree, I was!

MICHAEL: Nah, it was me.

WHO WOULD WIN A 5SOS WRESTLE?

CALUM: Ashton, for sure.

LUKE: Yep, definitely Ashton.

MICHAEL: Ashton would probably beat up all three of us. He's so muscular. I could never be that muscular.

ASHTON: I reckon between Michael and Luke, Luke would win. Between me and Calum, Cal would win.

WHO LOOKS BEST IN PHOTOS?

MICHAEL: The other three.

LUKE: It depends on the day, but I'm going to say Ashton.

CALUM: I'd say Luke.

ASHTON: Probably Luke. He's a good-looking dude, which is lucky because he's the guy in the middle on stage. Cal and Mike look good in photos too, actually. I don't think we've ever learned how to take really good photos, though.

WHO LOOKS THE WORST IN PHOTOS?

ASHTON: I think we all have our days. Especially when we're tired and we've been on tour for a few weeks.

CALUM: Probably me.

LUKE: Me.

MICHAEL: Nah, it's definitely me.

MICHAEL GORDON CLIFFORD

TWITTER: @ Michael5SOS

DOB: 20 November 1995

STAR SIGN: Scorpio

ASHTON FLETCHER IRWIN

STAR SIGN: Cancer

FAVORITE EMOJI: The monkeys.

DOB: 7 July 1994

TWITTER: @Ashton5SOS

FACTS &

STYLES

DOB: 16 July 1996

STAR SIGN: Cancer

TWITTER: @Luke5SOS

FAVORITE EMOJI: The one that's smiling with its teeth and has its eyes closed.

LUKE ROBERT HEMMINGS

CALUM THOMAS HOOD

DOB: 25 January 1996

STAR SIGN: Aquarius

TWITTER: @Calum5SOS

FAVORITE EMOJI: The eyes.

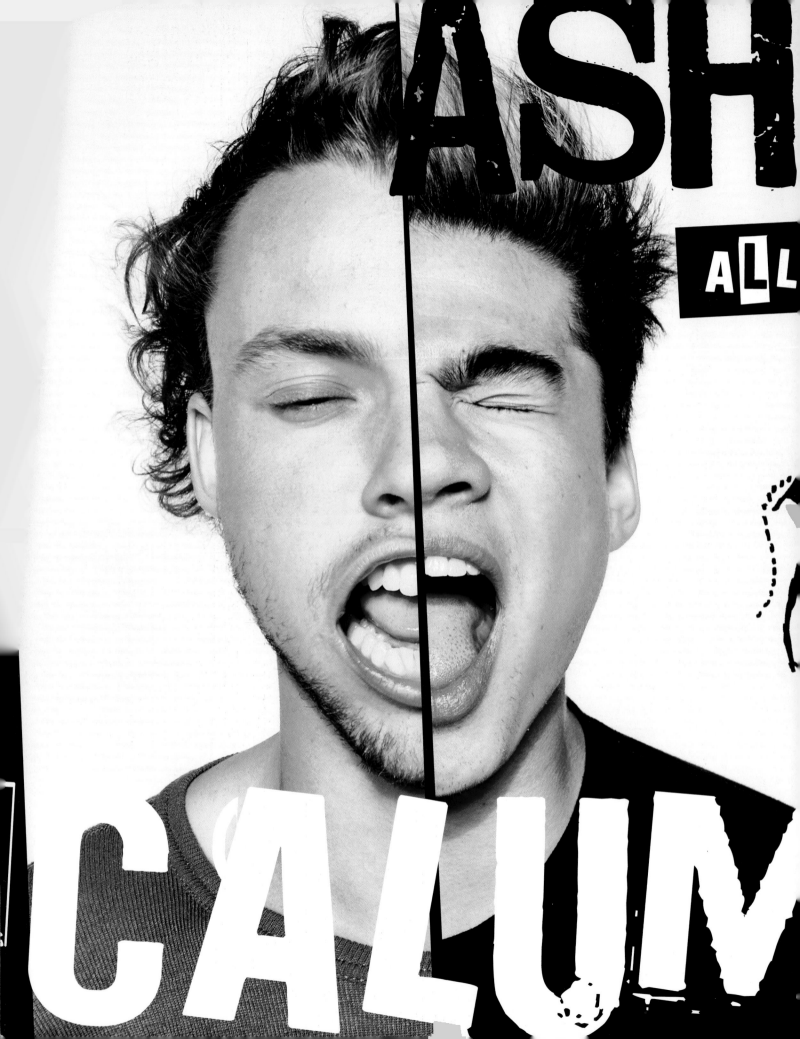

ASH
ALL

CALUM

ASH

WHAT'S YOUR FAVORITE 5SOS SONG AND WHY?

I love the song "Beside You" for a couple of reasons. One, because we wrote it about three and a half years ago when we were just starting out, and two, it's still one of my favorite songs to play live. I have a big connection to the track because it's about something important that was going on in my life at the time.

HOW LONG DID IT TAKE TO WRITE?

A few days or so.

DO YOU ALL HAVE TO WORK REALLY CLOSELY WHEN YOU'RE MAKING MUSIC?

We all have an equal part in writing and recording our music, and we're even producing on the next album. It's been a big part of this whole journey.

WHERE DO YOU DRAW INSPIRATION FROM WHEN YOU SONGWRITE?

Everywhere. I think it's important to self-motivate and go out and live life. It's a wonderful world and it's important to see it. I think the world itself fuels inspiration.

DO YOU EVER DISAGREE ON THINGS WHEN YOU'RE IN THE STUDIO?

Yeah, of course we do, but that's just because everyone's so passionate about what we're doing. Our sound is super-important to everyone, so people fight for their ideas. I think a big part of being in a band is about learning how to work together. You have to learn how to express your ideas to everyone without being aggressive. You also have to understand three other human beings, and it really is like having three brothers. You need to be able to see their points of view and get along. These are some of the most important things.

CAL

WHAT'S YOUR FAVORITE 5SOS SONG AND WHY?

Mine would probably be "Disconnected" just because it's so different to everything else. It has a lot of groove, so it's good to play as a bassist. I really like the melodies and stuff.

HOW LONG DOES IT TAKE TO WRITE A SONG?

It depends. It could take a couple of hours or it could take a few days. Usually it's just a day, but that can last from midday to midnight.

HOW DO YOU COME UP WITH SONG IDEAS?

I feel like we have to live first before we write songs. If we're not inspired by anything it's hard to be creative. So we go out and party a lot and take everything in, and then go into the studio and feel much more creative.

DO YOU EVER HAVE CREATIVE DIFFERENCES OVER YOUR SOUND?

Yeah, definitely, but it's quite an easy thing to get over. We all know it's not a personal thing, we just have pretty strong opinions. At the end of the day we want our music to be the best it can possibly be for both us and the fans.

57

ALL ABOUT THE MUSIC

LUKE

LUKE

WHAT'S YOUR FAVORITE 5SOS SONG AND WHY?

I really like a song called "If You Don't Know," which was on our EP. Me and Cal wrote it and I think it got overlooked a bit because of all the other songs, but I think it's cool.

HOW LONG DID IT TAKE TO WRITE?

It kind of came together in a few hours. I think it's a really relatable song.

WHAT INSPIRES YOU TO WRITE?

It depends on the song. We're all songwriters, but if it's just two of us writing a song then sometimes we'll craft it without the others and then we'll take it into the studio and everyone will have their input. The song may already be written, but it doesn't come to life until we're all singing it.

DO YOU OFTEN WRITE WITH THE OTHER GUYS?

We kind of go off in pairs and write songs, and then we all come together and choose all the best ones we've written from those two groups. Then we'll go into the studio and all put a new spin on it together.

DO YOU EVER CLASH?

I mean, you're always going to clash a bit, but I think that makes for a better recording. If you didn't clash the music would be average. But because everyone has such strong opinions and ideas, we bounce off each other. We never properly argue, though. It just doesn't happen.

MIKE

WHAT'S YOUR FAVORITE 5SOS SONG AND WHY?

"Wrapped Around Your Finger." It's a really special song to me and it's great to perform live because it's atmospheric and there are lots of good sound bites.

HOW LONG DID IT TAKE TO WRITE?

Luke and I wrote it together and it only took a few hours. For some reason it came to us really fast. We were trying to find our way with it, and something clicked and it came out sounding really cool.

WHERE DO YOUR IDEAS COME FROM?

It can be anything. Even seeing a couple of words on a billboard or hearing a melody can spark something. We might write the song one day and then the next week we'll all jump in with guitars and drums and stuff, so we always work really closely together.

IS THERE EVER ANY BICKERING WHEN YOU'RE RECORDING?

Honestly, not too much. I feel like there should be more, but I'm not complaining! We've always been really close and we still are. We sat together for four hours the other evening and just talked about nothing but music. After everything that's happened with the band, the fact that we can still do that is a great thing.

Thank you so much for always being there. You've made all of this happen and we couldn't be more grateful.

YOU ROCK
OUR WORLD

LOVE, 5SOS

THANK YOU!

★ ★

5SOS

YOU ROCK OUR WORLD

Library of Congress Control Number: 2015947632
ISBN 978-0-06-242450-1 (pbk.)
15 16 17 18 19   PC/RRDW   10 9 8 7 6 5 4 3 2 1
❖
First Edition

5 Seconds of Summer assert the moral right to be identified as the authors of this work

While every effort has been made to trace the owners of copyright material reproduced herein and secure permissions, the publishers would like to apologize for any omissions and will be pleased to incorporate missing acknowledgments in any future edition of this book.

© One Mode Productions Limited 2015

Photography on pp. 2-3, 4-5, 6-7, 8-9, 18, 26, 29, 32, 35, 42, 54-55, 56, 58, 62-63 courtesy of Tom Van Schelven. Photography on pp. 11, 15, 17, 20, 22, 24, 36, 40-41, 50 courtesy of Liz Hemmings. Photography on pp. 10, 12, 16, 21, 25, 28, 39, 43, 44, 50, 51 courtesy of Dee Christensen.

Text: Jordan Paramor
Illustrations and doodles: Rich Andrews
Design: Ben Gardiner